SO YOU REALLY WANT A DOG?
A Kid's Guide to Getting a Dog

Learn What You Need to Know to Show Your Parents You're Ready

Lynn Mills

Copyright © 2017 Lynn Mills

All rights reserved, including the right to use or reproduce this book or portions thereof in any form whatsoever without written permission from the publisher except in the case of brief quotations embodied in critical articles or reviews.

All photographs are used under license from Shutterstock.com.

Cosworth Publishing
21545 Yucatan Avenue
Woodland Hills CA 91364
www.cosworthpublishing.com

ISBN: 978-1-970022-26-1

For information regarding permission,
please send an email to *office@cosworthpublishing.com*.

Dedicated to Cosworth, Striker, Spot, and Woofer

So, you want to get a dog?

Of course, you do.

Dogs are fun and full of love, and they're always ready to play.

Some dogs like to go on hikes.

Some dogs like to swim.

Some dogs like to play fetch.

Some like to play tug of war.

Dogs make great friends. You can tell them your secrets and always be sure that they won't tell anyone else.

And when you come home from a long day at school and your dog greets you with a wagging tail and a smile, you can't help but smile, too.

So, you really want a dog? What's the holdup?

Your parents? Or your grandparents or guardians or whoever takes care of you? Just like taking care of you, taking care of a dog is a big responsibility. They may not be quite sure you're ready for it. They may be afraid that they're going to have to take care of you *and* your dog, too. Right?

First of all, get one thing straight — you will not be a "dog owner." You will be a "caretaker" to a dog. Are you ready to take care of a dog?

Answer the following questions to find out.

1. Just like you, a dog needs to eat every day. Sometimes twice a day. Do you:

    a. Let your dog learn to cook by watching *Top Chef*.

    b. Give your dog a Cheesecake Factory coupon and the keys to the car.

    c. Open a bag or can of dog food and put it in the dog bowl yourself. You said you wanted a dog.

2. Just like you, a dog always needs to have water to drink. Do you:

   a. Pop open a bottle of Perrier and hand it to him.

   b. Turn on the sprinklers outside and tell him to open wide.

   c. Keep fresh clean water in the dog's water dish every day, all day. You begged for this dog.

3. Now that your dog has eaten and had water, he or she needs to poop and pee. Do you:

   a. Tell your dog to cross his or her legs.

   b. Give your dog a magazine and show him or her where the bathroom is.

   c. Let the dog out in the backyard, or take him or her out on the leash. That's your dog.

4. But it's the middle of the night… or it's raining… and your dog is barking to be let out. Do you:

   a. Ignore the barking and go back to sleep.

   b. Tell your mom and dad to let the dog out.

   c. Come on… get up and let your dog out yourself. You said you could handle this.

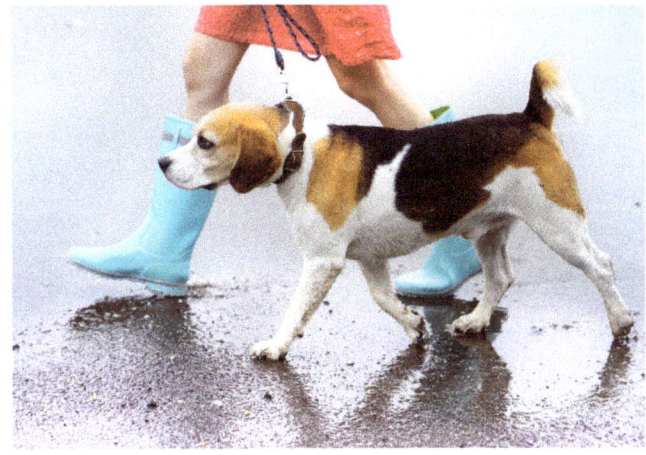

5. Uh, oh. You waited too long. Your dog made a poop in the house. Do you:

   a. Call the Hazmat Team.

   b. Move the couch over it. No one will notice a thing.

   c. Just scoop it up with paper towels, throw it away and wash your hands. And if the floor is wood or carpeting, ask your mom or dad what to use to clean it.

6. Chewing on stuff is a major dog thing. You wake up one morning to find that your dog chewed up your mother's favorite pair of boots. Do you:

   a. Frame the cat for it.

   b. Hide them and say, "What boots?"

   c. Admit what happened, and offer to do extra chores to earn money to replace them. From now on, make sure the dog can't reach any more shoes or boots and buy some chew toys.

7. Dogs eat lots of things they shouldn't, like your toys and dirty clothes. You come home from school and find that your dog ate the dirty, smelly socks and underwear you left on the floor. Do you:

   a. Figure it's great — less laundry to do.

   b. No problem. Just wait till your birthday. Grandma always gives you socks and underwear for your birthday… (yeah, thanks, Grandma).

   c. Watch to make sure your dog either throws up or "passes" the clothes. If he or she doesn't and/or seems ill, call the vet right away. Dogs can get very sick from eating non-food, so put your toys away and your laundry in the hamper where your dog can't get to them. Your mom wants you to do that anyway and now you have another good reason.

8. You just fed your dog. It was the right amount, but your dog still looks hungry. Do you:

   a. Give your dog seconds, and if he or she still looks hungry after that, give thirds and fourths until he or she stops looking at you with those big, cute puppy dog eyes.

   b. Let your dog go outside to hunt for himself or herself.

   c. Don't be suckered. Dogs always look hungry. Give your dog a doggy treat, but don't load him or her up. It's not healthy for a dog to be overweight.

9. Your dog likes to hang out at the table at dinner time. He or she whines for food and eats scraps that fall on the floor, which annoys everyone. Do you:

   a. Sneak your dog the veggies you don't want to keep him or her quiet. If they're good for you, they're good for your dog, right?

   b. Give your dog a little chocolate for dessert — you love chocolate, too, and he or she is making you feel guilty.

   c. NEVER FEED YOUR DOG "PEOPLE FOOD," ESPECIALLY CHOCOLATE. SOME DOGS GET EXTREMELY SICK AND COULD EVEN DIE IF THEY EAT EVEN A LITTLE BIT OF CHOCOLATE. If you can't train your dog not to beg while you are eating, put him or her in another part of the house during meals.

10. Your uncle thinks it's funny to put beer in the water bowl to get your dog tipsy. Do you:

   a. Take video. Your uncle's right — it's hilarious!

   b. Let him do it, but look at it as a science experiment.

   c. Tell him to please stop, beer is not good for dogs. Then wash out the dog's bowl and put water in it.

11. A dog needs exercise to stay happy and healthy. Do you:

    a. Get your dog a membership at the local gym.

    b. Get your dog a treadmill.

    c. Run around with your dog, play fetch, or go on walks together. You're a kid — play is your specialty. You can figure this one out!

12. You're trying to train your puppy to walk on a leash, but he or she just wants to pull and drag you. Do you:

   a. Let your dog go where he or she wants to go — just hang on tight!

   b. Never walk your dog again. He or she is not listening to you and it hurts your feelings.

   c. Try lessons at an obedience school or work with a good trainer. Many parks have free dog training classes. Keep working and stay patient — walking your dog is fun and healthy for both of you.

13. You've worked with your dog and he or she is well-behaved on walks but pulls and barks ferociously when another dog walks by. Do you:

    a. Let the dogs have at it. You know yours is tougher.

    b. Hold the leash tightly and keep yelling, "NO!" loudly until you drown your dog out.

    c. Hold your dog tightly, firmly say, "No," and keep walking past the other dog. Soon, your dog will learn not to bark when he or she sees other dogs. Praise your dog so he or she understands how to behave on the street. You've got this.

14. When guests come over, your dog gets excited and jumps on them. Do you:

    a. Shrug and say — "Sorry. That's just what dogs do" — and hope your dog grows out of it.

    b. Give your dog a stern "talking to" after the guests leave.

    c. Correct the dog when he or she jumps on anyone. Pull your dog away firmly, and calmly say, "No." Be sure to be calm, so your dog doesn't get even more excited. Do it every time. Your dog will get the idea soon.

15. Your dog is usually well-behaved, but sometimes makes a mistake — chewing on a shoe, digging a hole in the yard, etc. Do you:

   a. Beg your dog to stop doing what he or she is doing.

   b. Throw up your hands, figure your dog is untrainable, and just give up.

   c. Be patient. Try to catch your dog in the act and firmly say, "No." If you yell at your dog later, he or she may get confused. Sometimes dogs misbehave because they are bored and have extra energy. Try to exercise your dog more.

16. You want to play fetch, but when you throw the ball, your dog won't chase it. Do you:

   a. Start playing fetch with a boomerang.

   b. Chase after the ball yourself and bring it back in your mouth to teach your dog how the game works. He or she will get it some day.

   c. Not all dogs like to play fetch, so try to find something else to play. Some prefer tug of war with a rope toy, some like to run, some like to swim, some like agility training. Some just want to snuggle while you watch TV. Get to know your dog.

By now you know that C is the right answer to every question. Did you answer C every time? Then you know a lot about what it takes to take care of a dog — the feeding, the watering, the walking, and the playing. But there are a few more things to know about...

COMMUNICATION

Even though you don't speak dog and your dog doesn't speak human, you can still communicate. Get to know your dog's special barks and body language when he or she wants to be fed, or let out, or played with. Dogs usually don't understand words outside of the commands they have been taught, but they do understand your tone of voice. In time, you will be able to "understand" each other and you will both be happier.

HEAT AND COLD WEATHER CARE

Your dog is wearing a fur coat every day! Help him or her keep cool in the summer with shade, air conditioning and, of course, plenty of water — to bathe in and drink.

Never leave your dog in a car on a hot day, or even a warm day. Remember, it's much hotter inside the car than it feels outside. Cracking open a window or two won't help.

In winter, even with that fur coat, you still need to keep your dog warm when the weather gets very cold. Some dogs with thin coats even need sweaters.

TRAINING

You will need to teach your dog basic commands like "sit," "come," and "stay," so that he or she learns how to behave. You want your pup to be a nice addition to the family, not a problem. You can teach your dog to respond to spoken commands, hand gestures, and/or claps.

Give your dog one command at a time or he or she may get confused. Use a calm, firm voice. Don't yell at your dog — you wouldn't like it if your teacher yelled at you!

When your dog does what you ask, praise him or her. Give him or her a treat, too — your dog will be more likely to do it next time.

Remember that it takes time. You need to work with your dog often. And don't give up. Some dogs get it faster than others, but all dogs can learn new tricks — even older ones!

GROOMING

Dogs need to stay clean and groomed, so you will need to brush and bathe your dog. Some dogs like getting wet, others don't. You can pretty much count on getting soaked yourself. Or you can take your dog to the groomer and let them do it.

If your dog sheds a lot, you also need to groom your house — it's a good idea to get into the habit of sweeping or picking up the hair clumps off the floor when you see them.

HEALTH

To stay healthy, your dog needs to go to a veterinarian for check-ups, as well as shots for things like rabies and bordetella.

Since your dog can't tell you when he or she is feeling sick, you need to pay attention to changes in your dog's behavior. If he or she seems to be less active, is limping, is licking a certain spot, is eating less than usual, or is throwing up, those are signs to get your dog checked out by the vet. Sometimes you can just look into your dog's eyes and see that he or she is feeling sick. It's up to you to help keep your dog well!

OTHER PETS

You need to help your new dog and any pets you may already have get used to each other. It's a good idea to get tips from a dog expert, like your vet, on the best way to introduce them. Feed them in separate areas and make sure they don't get into each other's toys and beds. And never leave them alone together until you are sure they accept each other. Most importantly, give each one the same amount of attention so that they don't get jealous of each other. You want to be one big happy family!

THE PACK

Dogs are social animals. When you're home, your dog will want to hang out with you. When you are gone, he or she will patiently await your return and happily greet you when you come back home. You'll need to spend quality time with him or her, aside from the feeding and walking and other daily caring duties. Like any friendship, you get back what you put into it.

Wow, there's a lot of stuff to know about taking care of a dog, isn't there? So, do you still want a dog?

If you do, fill out the Certificate at the end of this book, showing that you are 100% ready, willing, and able to handle a dog. Sign it and give it to your family — it may not do the trick, but it might help.

MY CONTRACT WITH MY DOG

I _____ [insert name] pledge that I will take care of you.

I will play with you.

I will exercise you.

I will give you food and water.

I will make sure you get to the vet when you are sick or hurt.

I will not pull your tail or ears.

I will be your best friend.

MY CONTRACT WITH MY WONDERFUL PARENTS

I promise that if you _____ [insert name] allow me to get a dog, I will do everything I can to take care of him or her.

I will feed my dog and I will make sure my dog always has water.

I will let my dog out to poop and pee.

I will make sure all doors and gates stay closed so my dog can't get out and get lost.

I will train my dog to behave.

I will play with my dog.

I will tell you whenever my dog is sick.

I will bathe and brush my dog.

I will always love my dog. (I *really* want a dog!)

Signed,

_____ [insert name]

Now it's time to choose your dog. Choose carefully — this is a big commitment that will last your dog's lifetime. You want to make sure you pick the best best friend you can!

Don't choose a dog just because it's the most popular breed at the time, or you saw a dog just like it on a TV show. Read dog books and websites to see which would be the best fit for your family, your home, and your lifestyle. Talk to friends and relatives who have dogs and get their advice.

When you go to the shelter or rescue or breeder, or wherever you plan to get your new friend, check out a lot of dogs and pick the one you connect with — one that seems to like you, too. Yes, sometimes the dog will pick you!

Dogs are a kid's best friend.

THE END

About Lynn Mills

Lynn lives in Southern California
with her family and a very special dog.

lm@bylynnmills.com

Reviews are always appreciated.

Also by Lynn Mills

Mariposita Summer
(English & Spanish)

Engelmann the Footloose Christmas Spruce

*The Suicide Dilemma:
Making a Better Choice*

OTHER BOOKS FOR KIDS FROM COSWORTH PUBLISHING
www.cosworthpublishing.com

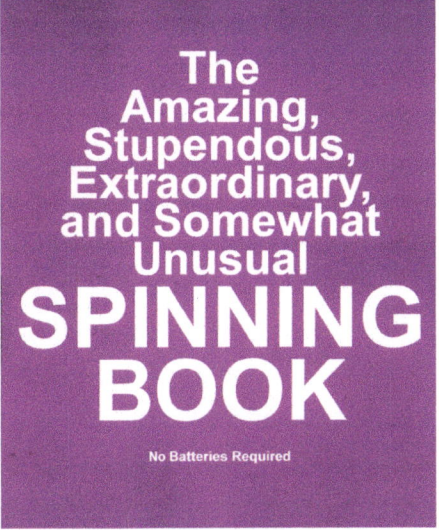

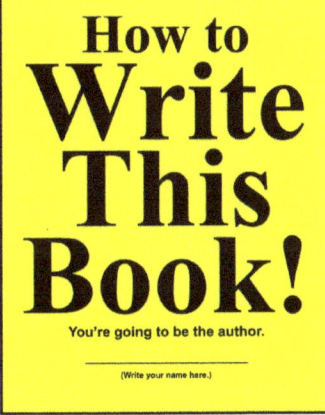

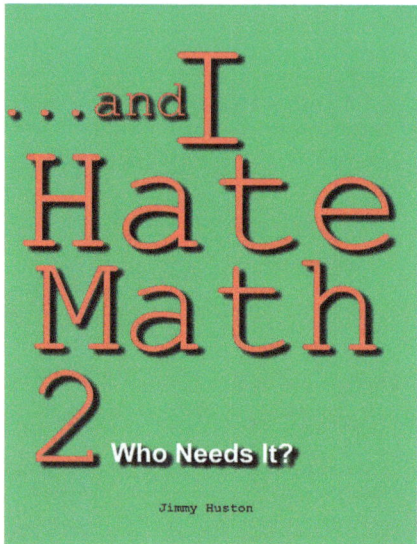

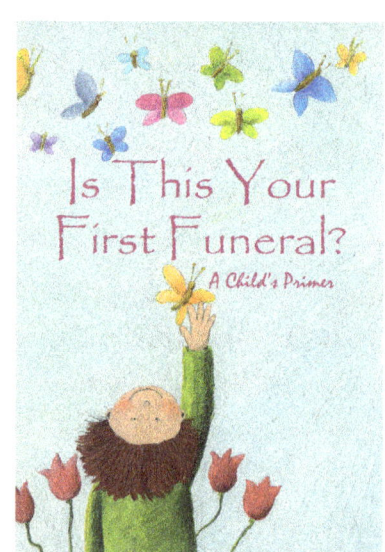

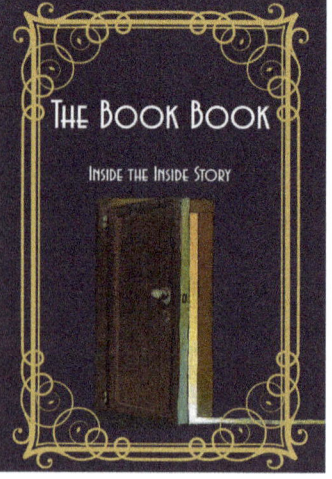

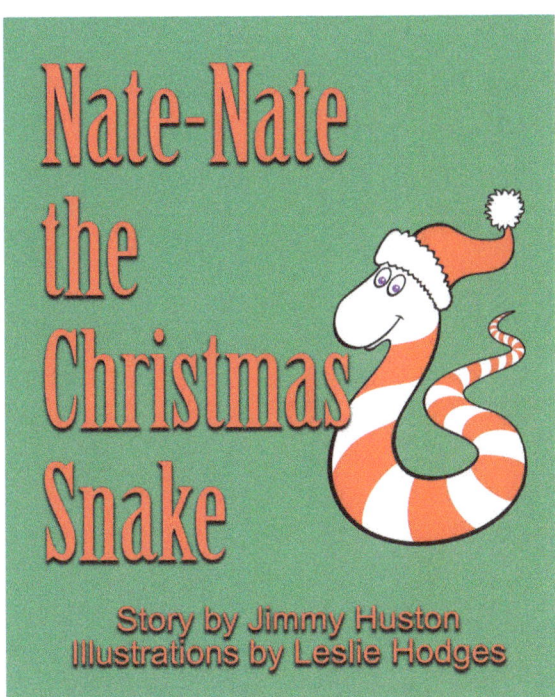

One of the very best new books about Christmas and reptiles!

Ripped from the headlines of Candy Cane Lane!

Follow little Nate-Nate as he explores Candy Cane Lane on Christmas Eve. He is not exactly welcomed by the neighborhood, but through his adventures Nate-Nate discovers the spirit of Christmas despite being a lowly snake in everyone's eyes.

When the joyful holiday mood is threatened, he slithers to the rescue and becomes the legend known far and wide as Nate-Nate the Christmas Snake.

No snakes were harmed in the writing of this book.

**NOW AVAILABLE AS AN
AUDIOBOOK FROM AUDIBLE.COM
Read by Sean Philip Glasgow**

www.christmassnake.com

If you're reading this, you will not like this book. It's not for you.

This book is for all the people who are *not* reading this.

They won't like it either, but it's short.

They'll like that.

"I didn't actually read this book. If I had, I would have loved it — but I never will."
                                                                                  Billy

" 'Hate' isn't a strong enough word for me. I loathe reading. I don't even like looking at pictures — which there are none of."
                                                                                  Wally

"This isn't what I wrote about this stupid book."
                                                                                  Zane

"This is an excellent coffee table book, if your coffee table hates to read."
                                                                                  Solomon

"This book made my teacher cry."   David

"My son loved this book. He said it was delicious."
                                                                                  Mr. Jones

"THIS BOOK IS SO DUMB THAT I COULD'VE WRITTEN IT."
                                                                                  Jimmy

www.i-hate-to-read.com

Other Books from Cosworth Publishing
www.cosworthpublishing.com

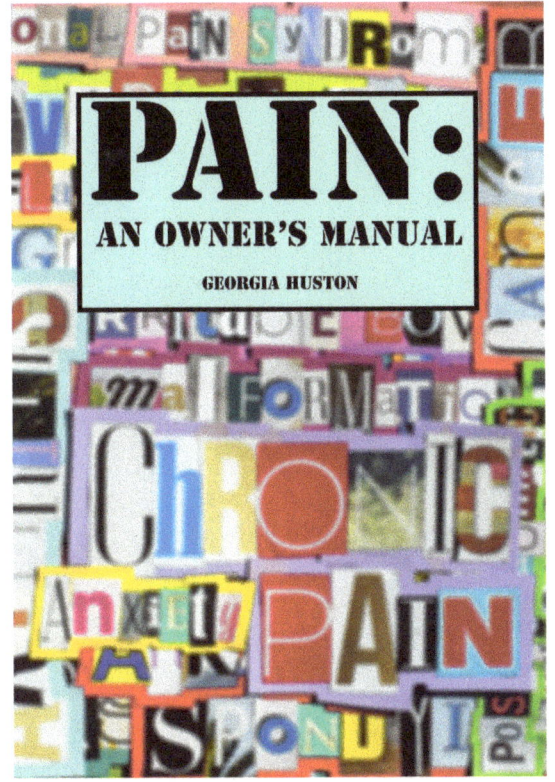
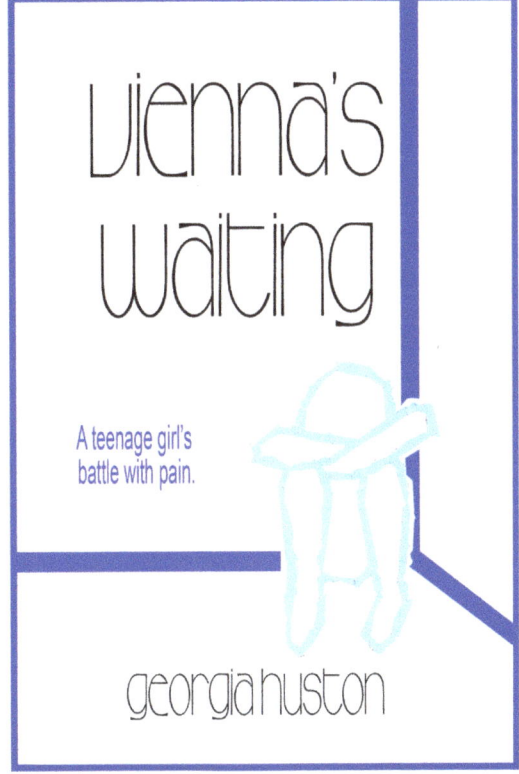

www.ingramcontent.com/pod-product-compliance
Lightning Source LLC
Chambersburg PA
CBHW040004080526
44586CB00027B/2875